THIS TENDER GEOGRAPHY

Cindy Williams Gutiérrez

FLOWERSONG

FlowerSong Press

McAllen, TX

FLOWERSONG
PRESS

FlowerSong Press
Copyright © 2024 by Cindy Williams Gutiérrez
ISBN: 978-1-963245-51-6
Library of Congress Control Number: 2024944173

Published by FlowerSong Press
in the United States of America.
www.flowersongpress.com

Set in Adobe Garamond Pro
Cover Image by Jessica Salazar McBride
Front Cover Design by Michael Kirshner
Back Cover & Typesetting by Priscilla Celina Suarez

NOTICE: SCHOOLS AND BUSINESSES

FlowerSong Press offers copies of this book at a quantity discount with bulk
purchases for educational, business, or sales promotional use. For information,
please email the Publisher at info@flowersongpress.com.

For my husband

In memory of my father

Lead back to the earth…
back to the body,
back to life.

—Friedrich Nietzsche

What I meant was all the colors
from ashes to singing.

—Li-Young Lee

Table of Contents

Acknowledgements

To my late parents, I acknowledge with deep humility and gratitude your devotion. In honor of the two of you who always remembered what was most present in the lives of others, in these pages I remember you. I thank you for your care and wisdom: You taught me the meaning of *boundless*.

To my husband, may you feel in your *kishkas* each line I write for you. And know that your uncontainable spirit lives in the spaces between the words.

To my sister, you pulse beneath my skin.

To Craig Santos Perez, for helping me shape these poems into journeys of discovery and this manuscript into a breathing place, I will always be grateful.

To Edward Viduarre of FlowerSong Press, thank you for believing in these words. Gracias del corazón for the first three words you shared with me after reading this manuscript.

First Tongue

My love is everlasting.
—my mother

Love, always,
—my father

Take gentle care,
—my sister

Map the first tongue to the geography of family:
words fueled by breath of four bordering bodies.
A hurricane of verbs: *need, protect, entwine.*
Soil with tended roots and a single shoot: *us.*
And an ocean of *everlasting, always, gently,*
breaking through narrow gulfs of silence.

To be raised beside a river is to be borderless.
When does a stream divide and when does it multiply
into a bridge? Where do you three end and I begin?
If I stop speaking, I hear your thrum in my lungs.
Your voice fills all my hollow spaces, the folds
of knee and elbow, shallow between collarbones.
Only fractions remain: wing, branch, wave.
I am not me without you, you, you.

Witness

"Don't look," my father croaked, "*I* won't."
The cat on the street was freshly dead.
I want to stare—hard—but don't,
except out of one yellow eye.

Years go by.
No friend has died of cancer.

I drive past a cat wrongly sprawled.
I don't stop, but I wonder if it's still
dying. If I were in my future, I'd turn back,
find out, then sit as long as it breathed.

As I Gaze at the World

His library has burned.
—Senegalese polite way of saying a man has died.

Cada cabeza es un mundo.
—Mexican proverb which means: *Each head is an entire world.*

My father was my resource to the world.
Whenever I had a question about anything,
I called him. He would say, *Give me a few minutes.*
There was no Internet, no Wikipedia, no Google.
Only the World Book volumes which he consulted,
along with his collection of history books—the Civil
War, the Titanic, the Spanish Conquest, the Mexican
Revolution—and his Enciclopedia Taurina expounding
treatises on bullfighting as the ballet of death.

Beyond storing countless facts in his head, he explored
the mysterious shapes of pyramids and yoga poses,
of numbers as ciphers. Numerology led him to decode
the holes riddling the body of history. He tracked
the specters of 4s hovering around JFK's assassination:
the date, temperature, hotel room, hospital name—
each sum to this number signifying *what could be
touched and felt.* I marvel at how my father made me
feel the meaning of his number, 9: *completion.*

But the stories occupying my father's private library
tugged harder at my imagination than integers.
Like Sheherazade, he wove sinuous tales
as if the sun refused to rise without them.
Each night as he kissed my brow, he never failed

to coax me to enter the places I yearned to be.
*Dream about Vancouver Island. Dream about South
Padre.* He seeded my imagination. When he died,
more than his library burned. The world was in flames.

Solstice Remembrance

Dusk.

I long to mourn my father's passing.
But the long days refuse the dark.

A breeze stirs the mallows, dormant.
Tight yellow buds unfurl into sunshine.

Dawn.

The green air whirs. Red petals pulse.
A lone hummingbird feasts on fire.

I awake in the middle of the night
and it is morning. Light will not leave me.

Siblings

At the end of Father's life,
there was little shade—

midwinter gaped.

Wooden, we stood
apart in our grief—

the last leaf fell.

Phantom Limbs

The tree lies at my feet like bones
of the razed house. I am caught
in its canopy-green cloud. Once,
in that cloud, I saw children
waiting for their father, watched
them run into his waiting arms.
Once I ran to my father,
stepped on the running board
of his VW bug. We circled
the cul-de-sac without stopping.
I was the first face that stopped him
when he arrived home. The first
beaming a long hello.
I climbed that unnamed tree
that is now a ghost, waiting
for my father. My father is
a ghost now. The tree is undead.
The green cloud reaches to the curb
where he parked the Volkswagen,
later the Valiant. Both washed-out grays
or the palest greens. The tree belongs
to someone else, to the new owner
of the unrazed house. The razing
is only in my mind. My father
is the trunk of the tree, the loam
for the roots of the tree,
the limbs spreading wide to the sun.
My face is my father's smile,
not merely undead, but radiant.
Memory is the name of the tree
no longer called ash. Only
the ash of wings still burning.

Ash still branching
into family with roots
in a place that can never be razed,
can never be ghost, never be lost.

Ghost Stories: Conversations with My Father

"He came out of nothingness, took form, was loved,
was always bound to return to nothingness."

—from *Lincoln in the Bardo,* a novel by George Saunders

I.
Imagine Lincoln—hair like ravens'
wings, eyes lit—with his son
in the bardo, this liminal state
before the union of marrow
with All—or Nothingness.

Enmeshed in the ashen
veil of the between-world,
this Abraham's son awaits
his father's tending to the son's
stillness, struck by whispered
words of love to the body
echoing with emptiness.

And the son, Willie, clutches
the veil, forgives its dust,
to remain in the bardo so long
as the father visits his grief
with murmur and touch.

II.
Imagine me with you, Father—
my bard—and the veil between us
visited by three words. The first—
enmesh—nets the grit of salt
or a chip of bone from your dust.

But *enmesh* unravels into nothing
when ash is not tendered into hands,
waiting. Grief's emptied body shrieks,
ravenous, from the unkindness
of loss. Without your silt sifting
through my fingers, only the *remains*
of love clutch—bind me to you.

In this marrow between worlds,
we map the *forgiving* topography
of touch—so long as we reach
through the dark, so long as I stroke
your features limned with light.

Primal

when ash stains your fingertips
with bone that fed your bone

        when silence is a blade
        keener than the screech of macaws
        slicing South Texas skies

                when the air is pockmarked   holes
                where the body that carried you within
                stood and moved and loved

keep breaking

        open   keep basking in the world
        because Willow greens your sorrow

                even now its canopy cradles
                your cracked body   its bole
                beckons your weary head

learn to weep

        funnel your rain into the river
        that surges to the sea
        that empties its mouth

                into this gulf of salt   but

churn toward the horizon

        where Ash is a tree that stains
        the air green   where macaw-
        shaped emeralds dazzle the sun

                              where clouds are made of bone

witness the infinite

                    end   no lament
                    but the confluence of every voice
                    keening in the celestial dark

                              each star a dry eye gleaming

Progressive Dinner

I.   Midnight Special with Elvis

Martinis, with a whole lot of shaking going on
Lazy Susan spinning in the center of the table
grace before we eat to land us in God's favor
main dish only thighs—
oh so close to the chicken's pelvis—
dancing before, during, and after—
your LPs, Elvis, were left for me under the tree
by Santa when I was his *baby girl—*
honey pie with a lemon twist

II.   Late-Night Supper with James Madison

In high school I wrote the Constitution with one cosigner—
Mr. Madison, my *founding father and I were neither forgers*
*nor plagiarists—*by hand on a scroll I scorched in the oven
tonight's menu on aged parchment, a quill pen,
and the right to choose
each course—naturally—by candlelight

III.   One More Meal with My Father

Tapas bar in Sevilla after a bullfight
shouts of *¡Ole!* and shots of tequila with salt
a pulsing *paso doble* and tales of matadors—
You played the bull as a kid with fingers for horns—
bites of Spanish tortilla and Serrano ham,
Manchego cheese, Manzanilla olives, Marcona almonds,
and the creamiest flan for dessert—
Your smile lighting the andalusite sky—
no leftovers: only forgiveness

Breaking

For my father

What if some wounds cannot be mended?
Some cracks spread below the surface.
Our glass hearts sewed *a parachute*
from everything broken. I want to breathe in
more than your vanishing. You said,
A break between us can bring us closer.

But what if once I swelled our distance?
Our dark undertow almost pulled us down.
Your hand quaked spontaneously as if to say,
A tremor has rippled across generations.
Most days we held each other upright.
A few lightless hours do not eclipse the rest.
Your scars were the pulsing stars on your skin—
now you are my dazzling underside.

The Bull

Hooves caught in motion,
does he dream of flames?
No, he gleams, fire-hued,

on my glass end-table—
his mosaic body muscled.
But he is lame. Missing

a horn and half a leg,
he reclines on his side.
My father rested easy,

after meals, in his chair,
reading, writing, napping.
Ringed by vitrines

of swords, sequined suits,
and slippers for the ballet
of death, my father dreamt

of facing the fiery, black
eyes of a brave bull.
He cried, *To be a matador*

is to dance with death,
and to live, charged
by the noblest creature. Mine

remains poised to thunder,
his sheared leg and horn
fusing in place on the pane

as if nothing were broken,
missing, or gone.

For My Sister Who Dreams of Blue Holes

A blue hole

ring of dove-

I want to freefall   emerge

Reef   dive   surface   dive

in this ice cave flooded

from this sinkhole to blue holes

the South China   the Dragon

cobalt   and sharks   bull   black-

not caged   gliding dangerously

a seemingly endless hole

this is where I want to sink now

just

the dark

in the Ocean as I Dream of the Sky

in the sky

tailing clouds

               near Belize in Lighthouse

                 and snag on stalactites

                   for millennia   I want to swim

                     in every sea   Caribbean   Red

                       Hole waits to be slayed   all this dark

                   tip   reef   nurse   hammerhead

                 close   this is the place I will find you

               made of two oceans   of silence

             in the right light   or with no light

touch

deep

Lorca's Lament

The sky charges into the sea
and turns into a frothing horn.
Only one blue: the bull of ocean.
The blade of horizon reddening.

Winged

she tosses and turns   flips over and over   her beak squeaking open   her eyes closed then
fluttering fluttering   as if trying to piece together her body her pain   the story of what
stunned her in midflight   her head droops   she stills   suddenly flaps her wings   skitters
no hobbles and the flipping begins again   I do not leave her   I cannot abandon this patch
of blue rug   I must witness a revival   can flight survive the clear hardness of glass   this
closed window insulating me from climbing temperatures   heat weights the air   air
should carry wings   she spreads her left   favors her right   this black and white
speckled fan refusing to open   my mother was turned from side to side in hospice
on her back she cried out *it's burning*   no time for thinning skin to crack   50
days of bedside vigil wasn't nearly enough   *death is a process* the hospice
worker said *it's a labor to let life go*   I told my mother stories about her
childhood   she once said *it's amazing how much you remember*   stories
I had gathered from her like feathers   I was building a nest of memories
twining them together so we could rest in their down   a place to
return   erasing the end for me   beginning again for her   wings
drafting behind those she loved   her father's antidote *give it time*
and the time he yelled ¡*Siéntate, Saltapared!* as she flitted back and
forth from the front seat to the back of the car   the way his scolding
mouth softened into a bird feeding its young   the worm his tale about
Saltapared   a beautiful little bird that jumps up and down   his favorite little
bird in fact   and the mouth-watering aromas in her mother's kitchen   tamales
de puerco con pasas calabacita arroz con pollo buñuelos menudo   and Mama's
proudest moments   the birth of her two daughters   the day my baby sister was
born I hid on the floorboard of our VW bug   my father parked in front of the Capitol
Records store   years later my favorite hangout   my father had an autographed
collection of Mexican LPs   it was the one thing I hoped he would leave me   he left me
alone in the car   no one under 14 admitted   I remember Mother waving to me from the
hospital window   dressed in a lacy white peignoir   from the third-floor window she looked
smaller than me   I could make out her smile   I didn't feel scared anymore   I sit in vigil cross-

legged by the French doors   the Three-Toed Woodpecker is too beautiful to die   am I too old
to cross my heart hope to die   I will her to recover from her dart into double-paned glass
I love the way breath fogs on glass   the way you can draw hearts or words in the mist of
breath   I was not there for my mother's last breath   her eyes closed   her mouth gaping
20 minutes can be a maw of time   I cannot take my eyes from the bird's thin tongue   all
I heard *thump eek eek*   the bird lolling on the patio   her long black beak too close to
the ground   she is my first sighting   I don't look in the bird book until after   I had
been listening to a talk about long-armed poems   what they sweep into their wake
of words   I witness the bird on the brink between waking and not   between
frantic and still   I missed the last moments of my friend Linda's life   I was ill and
didn't pick up my work line   it was the only number her husband knew to call
she wanted to see me   by the next day she was on the threshold   all I could
do   safeguard her passage   sometimes there are no words for what we do
I didn't guide my friend   but I wasn't beside the votive candle I had lit either
maybe I was closer to the threshold than I'd ever been   you see it was Linda first
then my father then my brother-in-law then my mother   pancreatic esophageal
lymphoma breast   and in between lung   my diagnosis   breath is a process   I was
lucky   I want this mama bird to be lucky too   does luck strike in threes   I can see
the three toes on her claw closing like a fist   fight little bird fight   my mother fought her
way out of a coma   one day she awoke sat up and spoke   she spoke all three weeks in
hospice   she even sang Happy Birthday with me to her caregiver   near the end her left arm
kept flitting up toward her head   and down again   a compass needle   a wing priming for

flight   my husband thinks the woodpecker's right wing is broken   I want her left wing to be enough   I want my mother's flitting arm to be enough   I want to be enough   I will not move from this spot   I watch her breathing   the bird's white breast crests and falls   she flips flips and flips again   heads tails heads   my father collected coins   and rocks and stamps and Mexican music   he did not leave me things   he did leave me   sometimes a different kind of leaving happens too near the end   a heart loses its way   how long before it reclaims its true north   we can meet at the threshold   maybe we carry the threshold within us   the day before my mother passed I left her side   I was reading her nest of stories   I was flying with her to the threshold   on currents of story and memory   little bird here I am   I am witness to your labor   my mother could no longer swallow   the hint of a rattle   the bird barely moves   but a burst of movement   the bird stretches   wings and claws reach toward something I can't see   her eyes open   she will surely take to the sky   stillness   I could have stayed that night   listened to the rattle deepen   regret is a ravenous wind   years devoured in seconds   you sit for 50 days and miss the last 50 seconds   if I live for another 50 years I want to live beside the threshold   astride the threshold   one wing joined with my mother my father   here one wing opening

Eclipse

The Greek personification of the moon is sometimes called Cynthia.

Darkness—the feral shadow strewn
across the radiant body—chills the earth.

The sun no longer speaks as the moon
reddens from the half-scowl of the earth.

Cimmerian winds fume into typhoon
until Cynthia's bow ushers light to earth.

I want to talk about breath   in and out and in   breath as a process   no way to possess breath   I want to talk about the memory of breath   how it remembers to flow   how it knows to take in the world   let it swell   ribs expanding breadth of understanding   I want to talk about breath   with word on breath air curling through nose and throat   lungs ballooning   diaphragm compressing vocal cords sounding new depths   with threads of thought   strings of memory and ribbons of poems unraveling now   I want to talk about breath   without breathing out   all this talking in my head   all these stories   movies running through the reel of my mind   I want to reel about breath   I want to reel from breathing in what's real   sun sky moon stars   and trees   remember to breathe the green of trees   rainforests feeding us   gifting us one more day   the tang of mangos   woodsmoke of embers   the brine of sweat-soaked skin   I want to talk about how we fail to remember   to count each breath   to calendar the exhale to celebrate each inhale   I want to talk about how we distance ourselves from breath   from the rattle of the last   as if this empty space makes it somehow easier to fill

A Meaningful Distance

between us, the heron pecks at a mass

of glassy seaweed, then ruffles its feathers.

The blue heron stands in the ocean's shallows

as wind slices the dunes. My ear pressed

to the sand, waves lap like timpani and

the pecking is plucked string. Now, the heron

dwells, rooted in the wet sand. My eye gazes

into its small sun.

                                                    Only us:

the heron, the tide, the clouds, and my right side

pressing into the sand, etching my shape onto grains

of earth that may be scorched into glass, into a vessel

to hold water or flame or feathers. I am a vessel containing

water and air. My lungs fuel breath and ignite a fire

beneath the weight of an anvil. Some call this asthma.

I call it

                                                        a silencing—

this metallic taste leaking from my chest. The gray-

blue heron lifts one lithe leg: grace balances. What

is the equilibrium between light and dark? My shadow-

stained lung compresses against the earth as my benign

left expands to inhale the lone heron's stillness. Breathing

stirs with ease. If

                                                        I refuse

anesthesia, will the heron peck the ground

glass from my right lung to keep—

at a distance—riotous growth?

Solstice Summons

Come, Jaguar, my feral guide,
shape-shifter
through the maw of night. Come

Artemis, huntress of the wild—
those with liquid eyes
slitting this shroud. Let me pierce

the longest dark, see the stark
beauty. Blanket me
with this shadow of the coming

end. Let me hear the hibernal roar,
its growling hunger.
Let me mouth grace, taste the dark

of my own raw heart.

Remedies

A broken heart: mend a split-rail fence, a fallen cairn; then darn a fleece blanket, a pair of alpaca socks

*

The war in your heart: sew a streamer of white flags, wave your prayer in the moonlight before you sleep

*

Shame: build a sand castle at high tide, paint family secrets on matchbooks, plant one in each turret, strike a match and watch—

*

Forgetting the ancestors: walk among weeping trees each day, rest beneath their canopies of shade

*

Miscommunication: practice gibberish with an invisible friend

*

Prolonged silence: sing on your balcony, in your meadow, from your rooftop

*

Saying too much: only touch

This Tender Geography

1. A lobe vibrates air
   Whole lungs can break into song
   Tumors make no sound

   A slope becomes a mountain
   I learn to breathe without you

2. I took root in you
   I tremor without your loam
   Clay mires my steps

   I inch toward a crevasse
   Both of you reach to catch me

3. You fear the ocean
   Water is my second skin
   You dwell in my deep

   Lambent rivers lure me home
   We tumbled from the same womb

4. Two maps of bodies
   This tender geography

We burn the same match

One breath feeds two mouths
Distance tenders into flame

How can I name what I did

"En somati" is Greek for "in the body."

what we do   lives   far   from words

it lies   in the body   *en somati*   in the in-   between

the empty space   stretching   from   what we touch   to   what we feel

how can I name   what I did   for my friend Linda   9 years ago   today

what is the term   for minding   a spirit   between worlds

I was not beside   her body   at her bedside   I was inside   her passage

I held the veil   open

no one knows this   but me   and now you   did she   feel   me

what do you call a husband   who abandons   his grief

to keep   his dead wife's   promise   her body   still   warm

Frank called   to tell me   she had   passed   only

15 minutes   after her last   breath   what name   can I give   to such an act

such generosity   his small breath   rattling   in my ear

did he run   to find her   the way   you found me

37

in Mendocino   that time   I didn't stay   where I said   I would be

        how did your body   lead you   200 miles   to mine

        how did her body   leave him   with no path   to follow

        there is no name for a compass   with no true   north

no term for shortness   of breath   while guiding   a friend   toward her last

and if   I call not to explain   it must have been asthma but to say   I have been thinking

       only   of you   and you say   you knew   I would call

       you felt it   since you   had been thinking   of me

            is there a name   for the moment   before I called

when the calling was heard   in the body   the gut   the bones

       and   is this more   fate   than   fact

when the Greeks point   to their bodies   north   of their core

       and say *phrane*   they mean   mind-and-spirit

       they mean   this mysterious   compass   pulses   in the chest

in yours   in Linda's husband's   in mine   even after   you are gone

     to learn to walk   after   after father   mother   friend   lover

            afterlife   is not   only   for the dead

Aubade for My Friend Linda

May you journey on a boat carved
of oak and rugged dreams left
varnished and shining on the horizon

May you be greeted by riotous rhinos—
irresistible to you—this parade of mothers
nuzzling calves with their tending armor

May you be served pasta with clams
the steamy dish you ate on your first date
the night you never left him—until now

May you take your father's hand—
pirouette as if the wind were your partner—
until your body curls into a child in his arms

Then dig your fingers in the loamy garden—
plant parsley for merriment, rosemary
for remembrance—and shimmer

in the darkest night, be our daybreak

Memorial Day

She wraps lilacs in newspaper and twine,
stuffs them in her baseball mitt.

Jogs barefoot, jeans scratching against snag
and fern. No cap today. The sun is blocked

by giant trees weaving diamonds of sky.
Crisp air and her throwing arm bristles.

The rest of the way, she plays blind
man's bluff. Soon a rickety fence.

She sucks the splinter, then the blood,
from her finger, eying the lone wooden

cross planted in the dirt across the field.
What to do when you're a cross between

a girl and a father's son. One by one, she pitches
the lilacs over the fence. They all fall

short of the mound.

The fact of the matter is

my friend's husband fell
in France, hit his head—hard.

> *It's elastic, this gray sponge*
> *crumpled in your skull,*
> *it stretches—did you know?—*
> *even as you age.*

A coma. Doctors mouth,
"There is nothing we can do."

> *Realign your hunch: the mad*
> *artist on the right, calculator*
> *on the left, conspire to lengthen*
> *their hold on fancy and fact.*

She pleas for prayers: votive-flames
arc through the void. Days break.

> *As your gait unsteadies, your brain,*
> *like a rubber band, can sling the shot*
> *of new vowels to your tongue,*
> *notes to your newly virtuosic hands.*

From across the Atlantic, she writes:
"The doctors say, 'He'll live.'"

You can learn to play a new
instrument, speak an unfamiliar
language, to extend the graying
mastermind, or—

Fall
to your knees.

Stranger at McIver Dog Park

You caught me at a strange time,
says the man, clean-cut, rifling
the ball to his dogs. They trail
a wake of dust as he confesses,
My father died nine days ago.
The man had buried a metal

ammo box with his father's last
photo and a pair of silver wings.
There, in the roots, nodding
at the gnarled fir nearby.
The dogs run toward the tree,
claw at the smoothed dirt.
I call it my Daddy Tree, his arms
opening toward the evergreen.

Ode to My Aussie Pup

When I watch you
cock your head,
your eyes—question

marks—track my every
move. When I watch
you sniff for hint

of hoof print and fur,
your muzzle tracing
the wild, I am dizzy

with musk. When I
watch your ears twitch
and perk at the distant

bleat, the rising tremor,
I vibrate with signals.
When I watch you prance

in hillocks of snow, burrow
your nose in flakes,
I could levitate. When

I watch you scramble up
the A frame, sprint through
tunnels, leap through tires,

I dream of reincarnation.

On a Summer's Day

One fly fisherman
in a blue float tube.
One brook trout, olive-brown.
Tiffany Lake.
A flock, Clark's nutcrackers.
Clouds, straying.
Sun, lazing.

On the bank,
one bench with a brass plaque.
A woman, skygazing.
Her drenched dog, black with copper points.
One pine tree, blacker, creaking—
a fire in the charred season
14 wilder summers past.

Where Eating Leads

Besides fire, I have consumed
dried apricots on the Bosphorus,
fleshy mangos in Manila, coconuts
on the milky sands of Ipanema.

I did not know dried fruit could be plump
as a glass of Turkish tea, leave no golden
strings between my teeth, taste as fresh
as shavings of vanilla-scented snow.

I have swallowed wind on the Seine and
the South China Sea, my hair pirouetting
off the port side of craft skimming
toward the Eiffel, casinos in Macao.

And I wolf down words, a craving long fed
by my father's midnight suppers of synonyms.
Soon eating was not enough. I began to exhale
gales of words onto the briny page.

But you know this. You alone—Muse, lover,
astonisher—testify to my indulgence in feral
tempest and luscious fruit. You never wonder
how I devour fire: you, burn through me.

Déjà vu

It's the same one, this T-top
on a maroon 300ZX, my first
sports car—this red hartebeest
on wheels, only faster—
loosening my hair to the wind,
its tug electric as your hand
at the end of our first date
when you let go slowly—
finger by finger—
as if it no longer belonged to me,
and I tore my gaze from the blue
in your eyes and bore home
in my Z—a deeper burgundy
than the Alexander Valley Cab
we drank—and I swear the beast
never swerved, but my heart swooned
as if seeing for the first time
the blue of starlight
under *this roof of Heaven.*

Trees in Winter

Two trunks entwined
like tresses, like torsos:

their denuded silver branches
spiral toward lazuline skies,

their nexus glistening
with the girth of snow—

a swaddled infant
gleaming in the crook

of conjoined bodies,
no, a pale belly

pregnant with my poems,
your landscapes—

two leafless trees startle
the crisp air to bare

the tangle of ecstasy,
and winter's heft—

the frozen suspended
before the melt—conjuring

the precarious weight
of my hand against your waist,

palm wedded to your side
shimmering cold

and closer as you sleep,
the vanishing—

Note I Never Left You

As marrow was aspirated
from your pelvic bone

I could not breathe
too deep to fathom

the core of one body
my life without yours

To My Beloved on Valentine's Day and My First Cancer-free Anniversary

Crimson

maple

blade—leafy

veined hand—

pressed

to your rib

I offer you light

incarnadined

by my pulse

greening

my phantom

lobe—budding

and breathing

you

in

Unmapped

In our small country
I explore your wilderness
You blur my borders

Breaking

For my husband

What if the only perfection is repair?
The Kabbalist's *tikkun olam* restoring shards
of light that ruptured at the world's birth.
Or *Kintsugi,* the Japanese art of mending
shattered pottery with lacquered gold dust.
Does the radiant remedy ennoble our sins?

What of the deliberate mistakes: the garden
in a Persian rug disrupted not to offend God?
The Navaho *ch'ihonit'i',* intentional spirit line
bleeding at the borders. I am broken open—
a cry for gold dust. *Reach for me* are shards
of longing, slicing skin, until one of us draws near.
You say, *A breakdown can be a breakthrough.*
I want to say, *Lo siento, I feel it, I feel you.*

Apology

River is body, rippling
        headwaters, open mouth—
the Methow, the Columbia's
        voluptuous heft—feeding
the land where our bodies dwell,
        but what of the underground

river snaking along our bodies'
        heaving, bodies crawling
toward apology's deep waters
        tumbling sequestered light
so we may both see a new
        sun, star, aurora—only

our tethered underside—& words,
        rising phosphorescent, dislodged
from memory's sediment,
        mouth to mouth—yours, mine—
apology rippling until each
        body shimmers into fire

Migration

the thief in me absconds with light   the candle in my belly flickers   dims inside
my thick cocoon

~ ~ ~

you pierce my dark
with the blade
of your gaze
blue knives pin me
I am prey
or chrysalis
broken wing
or unraveling
lace

~ ~ ~

I am Monarch   and you   my Oyamel forest   in the highlands

Abies religiosa   sacred fir   you reach across   miles

to pull me   to a wetter   clime   I cannot fly

but I hover   allow you   to hold me   my gossamer   glistening in the canopy   of your hands   I erupt

into cloud   a thousand wings   v i b r a t i n g

Beyond Eclipsed

The name Cynthia derives from the Greek goddess
Artemis who was born on Mount Cynthus.

Cynthia's arrow refuses to harpoon
the white whale pulsing above the earth.

Emerging golden from night's cocoon
a lithe jaguar illumines the earth.

Sometimes the writhing body—hewn
from entwined lovers—eclipses the earth.

Paper Dream

The mind is the machine of everything.
—my mother

I don't know

who planted it in me   sun   sky   river   clouds

I feel the roots   tangled in my spine

the vine propelling toward my pulse

there are moments it sprouts gold into my throat

moments when I speak red-tipped words

it's all a dream

this ream of paper that writes the world

porous   permeable   to the ink

not by logic can this realization be won   there is no winning

here   no release from gravity   but the final return

a vine   reborn from a small seed   in the dream

but my twin has already made up her half-mind

that necessary cog of doubt

keeps the vine growing   winding around liver and kidney   wending its way skyward

past lungs and heart   through windpipe   to the true north of breath

this summer squall   in my maw   whips

blank wads into falling   red-edged snow

if only I could read blood   like ink   if only I could find the seed

to hide the seed   from this dream

bonded to paper

perishable and caught   in *the machine of everything*

if only the machine were sun sky river clouds

if only light   rain   on the perennial vine

Snow

You drift

into avalanche,

your heft pristine,
the closest

matter

to the soul—

the 21 grams

after the body empties.

You spin,

crystals whirled

into a host of white-

robed dervishes.

Your solidity

remains

unmired

until the mar

of tire, shoe, scat.

How to keep this grit

from the landscape

of my life?

Teach me

your Inuit names:

one to prevent

the melt

into maculate

terrain

and one sin-

fully near

this drift

of being.

More Remedies

Betrayal: remove ribbons from bodices, petticoats, and corsets; gather hair from wild horses; braid the frayed ends

*

Divorce: bake two loaves of bread and share both

*

Grief that lingers: lay calla lilies at the feet of an enemy

*

Loss of a parent: tuck one lesson your parent taught you in a fortune cookie every day; devour your good fortune on the anniversary of your parent's passing

*

Loss of the beloved: sketch the face you know by heart with kohl, then close your eyes before a mirror—each feature you have traced will appear on the backs of your eyelids

*

Approaching death: cast your own death mask; wear it on the eve of your birthday

First Thunder

Water carries memory.

—Acosia Red Elk

Babies must be 80 percent memory,
our bodies nearly as aqueous as the womb
where our hearts first thunder.
Infant remembers ancestor, carries the waters
of knowing in cell and capillary
until they are dammed in the hush to grow up.

And the forgetting begins: to float
in the placenta, free and fed, is only a blur.
To roil and drift, a figment, delirium.
So we dream of the sea outside the body.
We turn to the night sky for signs.
But time ransoms each sparkle and droplet:
we erase what we are—stardust, ocean.
Thunder anew—meteor, tsunami.

If I Text You Now

1. 02.02.11

    u taught me how 2 die
    with grace   u awoke
    & looked at ur self
    disappearing thru
    Frank's eyes   u saw
    my dear friend
    what it was TBF

2. 02.01.13

    some people see things
    hear things   all i want
    1 visitation   ur quiet
    & ur shouts of *Olé!*
    ur sea green eyes
    ICYMI i still write 2 u

3. 02.16.14

    there is no law above love
    u were simply brother
    u shared ur dying with us
    u always thanked us 4 coming
    will u the next time we meet
    thank u 4 saying IDK

4. 01.19.15

    i wish u would 3RB

i need u 2 breathe fully
i wonder what follows omicron

5. 12.10.15

    i still have ur ashes   thank god
    i interviewed u ur last 3 yrs   i
    call ur nest of stories lets keep
    talking   like u always used 2
    say   TTYL

6. Date UNK

    lets meet in a blue hole   lets
    find a way TBH   lets find
    the way 2 each other

7. Date UNK

    thx in advance   i dont want 2 later
    LMK what u need   i need u
    2 burn thru me   lets say it all
    now

Catalog of Unabashed Forgiveness

After Ross Gay

For not seeing the hole in you
For not seeing the lit whole of you
For eating to fill the ragged hole in me
For my voracious drive
For not learning how to drive stick until I lived in the sixth largest city in the world
For not sticking up for the orphans we become on the empty street where we meet
For staying stuck in the caliche of the past
For not starting over
For not giving myself over like surf ravenous for sand
For not taking risks
For risking too much on the edge of brash ice
For gambling with trust
For not trusting the voice in my gut
For rousing the rawness in my voice only in ecstasy
For not marrying a dancer
For not dancing beneath the willow in my meadow
For dancing tango only in the milonga of my mind
For unbridling the stallion of my mind
For not wilding the page
For reining in my untamed
For the times I choke on the bit
For not asking my father about his life
For not teaching my father how to reach me
For disappearing behind sheaths of silence
For not disappearing in a hot-air balloon
For not skygazing every day
For not gazing at clouds with my mother except when I was little
For wondering *Why am I here*

What do I want
Will I end up alone in the company of poems
Will I live in a treehouse instead of a box
What if I ran away with the wind
For asking too many questions
For tiring of people who never pose questions
For not learning how to change a tire
For not learning how to put chains on my tires while living in the North Cascades
For betting on breaking the chains handed down to us
For not insisting *things must change*
For not changing my mind
For not rearranging the furniture
For closing the door too soon
For not finding the door the window the fire escape
For leaving home
For never letting go of home
For rarely feeling at home
For straddling rivers of cultures
For leaving mine leaking at the door to the corporate world
For nesting alone in the redd
For longing for someone to see all the way down to the bed of my confluent streams
For longing for my mother and my father
For searching for my sister
For thinking I have found her in a friend
For forgetting she was my first friend
For never telling my mother she was my best friend
For not being the friend my father needed at the end
For shattering
For scattering the pieces into the wind

All I can do is *forgive myself the lot*
All I can do is *laugh and sing* a lot
All I can do is wipe clean the slate
Balance the scales in this fallen state
Open new territories of flaws and mistakes
Make room for the uncharted parts in me

Explore the holes the faults the tectonic breaks
The rugged terrain of this tender geography
And I ask you to *come, come, whoever you are*
You, *wanderer, worshipper, lover of leaving*
You, cleaver of vows a thousand times over
Indulge in it all—the giggling, the grieving—
Sink your claws in the clay of this rotating sphere
All I can do is invite us both to be fully here

Notes

"Ghost Stories: Conversations with My Father": In Tibetan Buddhism, bardo is the state of existence between death and rebirth. Coincidentally, many of my father's friends called him Willie, a nickname for his surname Williams.

"Primal": This poem is inspired by Claribel Alegría's poem "Lluvia" ("Rain").

"Breaking" (for my father): The first italicized line is taken from the poem "Any Time" by William Stafford. The thought in its entirety reads: "I have woven a parachute out of everything broken."

"Eclipse": In Greek mythology, Cimmerian refers to a mythical people who lived in perpetual mist and darkness near the land of the dead.

"A Meaningful Distance": Ground-glass opacity (GGO) is a radiological finding in computed tomography (CT) consisting of a hazy opacity. The incidence of cancer in GGO has been reported as high as 63%.

"Aubade for My Friend Linda": This poem was written for my dear friend and colleague Linda in tribute to her and all that she cherished.

"Stranger at McIver Dog Park": My humble thanks to the stranger who shared his story with me in the off-leash area of Milo McIver State Park.

"Déjà vu": The italicized phrases are taken from the opening and closing lines in "Hammer" by Christopher Howell.

"Unmapped": The idea of "the small country" came to me as I was musing on the notion of the tender geography of the body. This line is beautifully rendered by Ellen Bass in "The Small Country." Though Ellen's poem did not inspire mine, I am grateful to have read and studied her poem.

"Paper Dream": I cannot recall the source of the first italicized line in the poem. But I know it is not mine. All I can do is ask for forgiveness and offer my gratitude.

"First Thunder": My thanks to Acosia Red Elk for her wise teaching. The poem's last line is a nod to one of my favorite William Stafford lines: "Your job is to find what the world is trying to be," which is the closing line in the poem "Vocation."

"If I Text You Now": These are the acronyms used in the poem:
TBF = to be frank
ICYMI = in case you missed it
IDK = I don't know
BRB = be right back
TTYL = talk to you later
UNK = unknown
TBH = to be honest
LMK = let me know

"Catalog of Unabashed Gratitude": This poem is inspired by Ross Gay's luminous poem "Catalog of Unabashed Gratitude." The first two italicized phrases in the last stanza are borrowed from "A Dialogue of Self and Soul" by William Butler Yeats. The last two italicized phrases are from a poem by Rumi translated by A. J. Arberry. The poem begins "Come, come, whoever you are."

Source Acknowledgments

Grateful acknowledgment is made to the journals, anthologies and galleries in which some of these poems first appeared.

The following poems were published in *The Shrub-Steppe Poetry Journal:*

"First Tongue" (2024)
"Solstice Remembrance" (2024)
"Phantom Limbs" (2024)
"Where Eating Leads" (2023)
"The fact of the matter is" (2021).

An excerpt of "Witness" was published under the title "Bearing Witness" in *In the Mist: Giving Voice to Silence* (NotaBeast, 2015), alongside photography by Russell J. Young.

"Ode to My Aussie Pup" appeared in the anthology *Cats and Dogs Reining* (Shrub-Steppe Poetry, 2020).

"Remedies" was printed in the postcard set *Uncertain Times: Poems of Healing and Refuge* (Confluence Poets, 2021).

The following poems were exhibited in the collaborative art exhibit "Inspired" at the Confluence Gallery in Twisp, Washington in 2023:

"For My Sister Who Dreams of Blue Holes in the Ocean as I Dream of the Sky" (in collaboration with illustrator and papercut artist Hannah Viano)

"Paper Dream" (in collaboration with painter Michael Kirshner).

About the Author

Poet-dramatist Cindy Williams Gutiérrez was awarded the 2018 Willow Books Editor's Choice Poetry Selection and a 2016 Oregon Literary Fellowship for *Inlay with Nacre: The Names of Forgotten Women*. She was selected by *Poets & Writers Magazine* as a 2014 Notable Debut Poet for *the small claim of bones*, which placed second in the 2015 International Latino Book Awards. Cindy received the 2017 Oregon Book Award for Drama for *Words That Burn*. In 2022, she co-produced her choreopoem, *In the Name of Forgotten Women*, which was acclaimed by Portland's *Willamette Week* as "a vibrant call for action."

Cindy has taught poetry to youth in every grade from K-12 in Washington and Oregon and is currently a teaching artist at Paschal Sherman Indian School on the Colville Reservation. She is cofounder of El Grupo de '08, a Northwest collaborative-artists' salon; Los Porteños, Portland's Latinx writers' collective; and the Confluence Poets in Washington State's Methow Valley. Along with an MBA and an MA in International Studies from the University of Pennsylvania's Lauder Institute, Cindy earned an MFA from the University of Southern Maine Stonecoast Program with concentrations in Mesoamerican poetics and creative collaboration.

Cindy is inspired by the silent and silenced voices of history, herstory and her own story. She dreams of the day when history will expand into ourstory.

Advance Praise for
This Tender Geography

Cindy Williams Gutiérrez is one of my favorite contemporary poets. Her work tenderly explores the deep geographies of family, friendships, the environment, and human-animal relations. Throughout, she maps the thresholds of loss and love through carefully crafted narratives and haunting images. Every page feels like an ocean of emotions breaking open; at the same time, every page is "one wing opening."

—**Craig Santos Perez**, 2023 National Book Award Winner for Poetry
and author of *From Unincorporated Territory [åmot]*

Like putting pushpins into a map of longing and desire to find her way home, Cindy Williams Gutiérrez's *This Tender Geography* is a book of attention, precision, and wonder. Her hold on the subjects of illness and death is poignant. Her care for the subject of love is pierced with wonder. Some of this book's poems are entangled in passion. Others move toward restraint. But, all the poems in this wonderful book glow with Gutiérrez's evocative lyricism and graceful intensity.

—**David Biespiel**, National Book Critics Circle Balakian Award Finalist
and author of *Republic Café*

In *This Tender Geography*, the poet Cindy Williams Gutiérrez offers a series of carefully crafted meditations on love and loss. These poems offer a chance to consider our own relationships, and to think about how we fashion, tug, tear, and sometimes mend the web of life as we traverse it. Love is what renders us alive, the poet argues. In a brilliant sequence titled, *Remedies*, Williams Gutiérrez offers a variety of cures for as many ailments: for "Forgetting the ancestors," a walk among weeping trees, and for "A broken heart," mending a split-rail fence. This wonderful book, full of inventive forms and gratitude, is a sort of remedy itself for days when we might need a dose of beauty. Thank you, Cindy, for your words, for the care and tenderness you have poured onto these pages.

—**Claudia Castro Luna**, Washington State Poet Laureate (2018-2021)
and author of *Cipota Under the Moon*

If, as they say, when a dear one dies a whole library of stories has burned, then this book turns that lament to abundant creation—telling stories of the lost so they return to us, summoned by these poems. Cindy Williams Gutiérrez conjures family, story, and healing thought from the shadows in the spirit of "say it all now."

—**Kim Stafford**, Oregon Poet Laureate (2018-2020)
and author of *As the Sky Begins to Change*

FLOWERSONG
P R E S S

FlowerSong Press nurtures essential verse
from, about, and throughout the borderlands.
Literary. Lyrical. Boundless.

Sign up for announcements about
new and upcoming titles at:

www.flowersongpress.com